Sounds!

By J. Douglas Lee

Pictures by Lesley Smith

Gareth Stevens Publishing
Milwaukee

BRIGHT IDEA BOOKS:

First Words!
Picture Dictionary!
Opposites!
Sounds!

The Four Seasons!
Pets and Animal Friends!
The Age of Dinosaurs!
Baby Animals!

Mouse Count!
Time!
Animal ABC!
Animal 1*2*3!

Homes Then and Now!
Other People, Other Homes!

Library of Congress Cataloging-in-Publication Data

Lee, J. Douglas.
    Sounds!

    (Bright idea books)
    Bibliography: p.
    Includes index.
    Summary: Short sentences and special activities featuring alliteration, rhyme, and phonetic spellings introduce sounds and the words used to describe them and encourage the reader to respond creatively.
    1. English language — Onomatopoeic words — Juvenile literature. 2. Sounds, Words for — Juvenile literature. [1. Sounds, Words for. 2. English Language — Onomatopoeic words] I. Smith, Lesley, ill. II. Title.
PE1597.L43   1985   428.1   85-25197
ISBN O-918831-74-1
ISBN O-918831-73-3 (lib. bdg.)

This North American edition first published in 1985 by

Gareth Stevens, Inc.
7221 West Green Tree Road   Milwaukee, WI 53223, USA

Typeset by Ries Graphics Ltd.
Series Editors: MaryLee Knowlton and Mark J. Sachner
Cover Design: Gary Moseley
Reading Consultant: Kathleen A. Brau

Contents

SOUNDS! 4
In the Kitchen 4
In the Bathroom 6
In the Yard 8
In School 10
In the Playground 12
On the Street 14
At the Concert 16
In the Supermarket 18
On the Farm 20
In the Farmyard 22
In the Woods 24
By the Brook 26
At the Seashore 28
At the Circus 30
At the Zoo 32
At the Football Game 34
On a Train 36
A Stormy Day 38
In the Snow 40
Going to Sleep 42

Things to Talk About 44
Things to Do 45
Sound Off!: Index of Sound Words 46
More Books About Sounds 47

For Grown-ups 48

"Bubble, bubble," bubble Susan's boiling pots.

"Clang, clang," clang the pots and pans.

"Hisssss," steams the kettle.

5

"Splish-splash,"
splashes the water
in Bobby's bath.

"Click-click,"
clicks the light switch.

In the Bathroom

"Drip-drop," drips the tap.

"Zzzzzz, zzzzzz," says Eddie's electric shaver.

"Gurgle, gurgle," goes the gurgling water down the toilet.

In the Yard

"Slurp, slurp," sips Susan.

"Meow-meow," meows Bobby's cat.

"Purrrr," sigh the cute kittens.

8

"Chirrup, chirrup,"
chirp the cheery birds.

"Arf! Arf!"
barks Becky's dog.

"Bzzzz, bzzzz,"
buzzes the bumblebee.

9

"Squeeeeek! Squeeeeek!"
squeaks Susan's
squeaky chalk.

"Flip-flop,"
flops Becky's
floppy book bag.

"Scratch, scratch,"
writes Rhonda's pencil.

11

In the Playground

"Creak!"
sings out the swing.

"Boing!"
bounces Bobby's ball.

"Swish-swish,"
swings the jump rope.

"Ah-Rrrrr!"
wails the siren.

"Ting-a-ling,"
pings the bicycle bell.

14

On the Street

"Bleep-bleep,"
beep the car horns.

"Brrrrrmmmmmm,"
go the cars.

"Brrrrrupp! Brrrrrupp!"
hammers the jack hammer.

15

At the Concert

"Oomph! Oomph!" oompahs the tuba.

"Blare-blare," blow the trumpets.

"Boom, boom,"
bump the drums.

"Clash-crash!"
clap the cymbals.

"Ting-a-ling,"
tings the triangle.

"Jingle-jangle,"
jangles the tambourine.

17

In th Supermark t

"Whirrr-er,"
purrs the freezer.

"Rattle-rattle,"
rumbles Susan's cart.

"Click-clack,"
clacks the cash register.

19

"Squeee-squeee!"
squeal the swine.

"Ma-ooo!"
moo the cows.

"Hee-haw!"
brays the burro.

20

On the Farm

"Baa, baa!"
bleat the sheep.

"Clip-clop,"
clump the horse's hooves.

In the Farmyard

"Braaat! Cluck-cluck-cluck,"
holler the hens.

"Peep, peep,"
cheep the chicks.

"Cock-a-doodle-doo!"
crows the rooster.

"Sssss, sssss!"
hisses the goose.

"Gobble-gobble,"
go the turkeys.

"Whack-whack!"
quack the ducks.

23

"Who? Who?"
asks the owl.

"Snuffle, snuffle,"
sniffs the badger.

24

"Rush, rush," rustle the leaves in the wind.

In the Woods

"Caw, caw," call the crows.

"Cuckoo, cuckoo," cuckoos the cuckoo.

By the Brook

"Splish!"
splash the jumping fish.

"Whoosh! Whoosh!"
rushes the water in the brook.

"Blup!"
plops the thrown stone.

"Rivet! Rivet!"
croaks the frog.

At the Seashore

"Lup-lap,"
laps the water on the shore.

"Squawk!"
scream the seagulls.

"Chug-a-lug-lug,"
chugs the motorboat.

"Crash!"
go the waves.

At the Circus

"Aark-aark!" bark the seals.

"Boom-ba-boom," bangs the big bass drum.

"Blar-blar," blares the band.

"Snap!" cracks the whip.

"Hooray!" cheer the children.

31

At the Zoo

"Rrrr-rrrr!"
roars the lion.

"Thump! Thump!"
thud the elephant's feet.

"Grrr, grrr,"
growls the grizzly bear.

"Chitter-chatter!"
chatter the chimps.

33

At the Football Game

"Tweet! Tweet!"
trills the whistle.

"Crrruuunch,"
pile up the players.

"Popcorn! Popcorn!" pipes up the vendor.

On a Train

"A-whoo! A-whoo!"
blows the whistle.

A Stormy Day

"Whaa-ooo,"
howls the wind.

"Pitter-patter,"
pelts the rain.

"Crash!"
cracks the thunder.

"Clatter-crash!"
clunk the garbage cans.

"Swoosh,"
slide the sleds.

"Clack-clack,"
click the skates.

"Scrunch, scrunch,"
crunch Bobby's boots in the snow.

In the Snow

"Tinkle-tinkle,"
go the icicles.

"Splosh!"
slaps the snowball.

Going to Sleep

"Zzzzzz,"
we snore as we sleep until sunrise.

Things to Talk About

1. Most people know about sounds through <u>hearing</u>, which is one of our five senses. The other senses are <u>sight</u>, <u>taste</u>, <u>touch</u>, and <u>smell</u>.

   The pictures in this book name the sounds that most of us <u>hear</u> around us. But some of us do not always hear as well as others. That is why we need the other senses.

   Do you know anyone who cannot hear as well or see as well as most other people? Do you think this person makes up for this with his or her other senses? How can you tell?

2. See "On the Street" on page 14. Imagine that one of the people in this picture cannot hear all of the sounds on the street. How might this person use his or her sense of <u>sight</u> to know important things about safety in the street?

3. Find the picture of the football game. How can you use the sense of <u>smell</u> in this picture? How about <u>touch</u>?

4. Here are some places in this book where we hear sounds:

   *the seashore, *the farm, *a train, *the playground, *a stormy day, *the circus, *school.

   What sounds in these places do you like most? Which sounds do you like least? Can you say why?

Things to Do

1. See "In the Playground" on page 3. What sounds do the slide, roller skates, and seesaw make? Can you make these sounds?

2. Find a brother, sister, friend, or grown-up you know, and see if any of them can guess what sounds you are making!

3. Find the Index of Sound Words on page 46. See if there are any words in the list that look like the sounds you've just made.

4. Find the pages called "Going to Sleep." What is the only sound in the whole picture that the children are making?

   What else in the picture might also make sounds?

   What sounds would they make?

Sound Off!: Index of Sound Words

A
A-whoo 36
Aark-aark 30
Ah-Rrrrr 14
Arf-Arf 8
Asks 24

B
Baa 20
Bangs 10, 30
Bark 30
Barks 8
Beep 14
Blar-blar 30
Blare-blare 16
Blares 30
Bleat 20
Bleep-bleep 14
Blow 16
Blows 36
Blup 26
Boing 12
Boom 16
Boom-ba-boom 30
Bounces 12
Braaat 22
Brays 20
Brrring 10
Brrrrrmmmmmm 14
Brrrrupp 14
Bubble 4
Bump 16
Buzzes 8
Bzzzz 8

C
Call 24
Caw 24
Chatter 32
Cheep 22
Chirp 8
Chirrup 8
Chitter-chatter 32
Choo-choo 36
Chug-a-lug-lug 28
Chugs 28, 36

Clack-clack 40
Clacks 18
Clang 4
Clap 16
Clash-crash 16
Clatter-crash 38
Click 40
Click-clack 18
Click-click 6
Clicks 6
Clip-clop 20
Cluck-cluck-cluck 22
Clunk 38
Cock-a-doodle-doo 22
Cracks 30, 38
Crash 28, 38
Creak 12
Croaks 26
Crows 22
Crrruuunch 34
Crunch 40
Cuckoo 24
Cuckoos 24

D
Da-dum-da-dum 36
Ding-dong 36
Drip-drop 6
Drips 6
Drum 36

F
Flip-flop 10
Flops 10

G
Go 14, 22, 28, 40
Gobble-gobble 22
Goes 6
Growls 32
Grrr 32
Gurgle 6

H
Hammers 14
Hee-haw 20

Hisses 22
Hisssss 4
Holler 22
Howls 38

J
Jangles 16
Jingle-jangle 16

L
Laps 28
Lup-lap 28

M
Ma-ooo 20
Meow-meow 8
Meows 8
Moo 20

O
Oompahs 16
Oomph 16

P
Peep 22
Pelts 38
Pile up 34
Pings 14
Pipes up 34
Pitter-patter 38
Plops 26
Popcorn 34
Purrrr 8
Purrs 18

Q
Quack 22

R
Rah-rah 34
Rattle-rattle 18
Rings 10, 36
Rivet 26
Roars 32
Root 34
Rrrr-rrrr 32

Rumbles 18
Rush 24
Rushes 26
Rustle 24

S
Says 6
Scratch 10
Scream 28
Scrunch 40
Sigh 8
Sings 12
Sips 8
Slam 10
Slaps 40
Slide 40
Slurp 8
Snap 30
Sniffs 24
Snore 40
Snuffle 24

Splash 26
Splashes 6
Splish 26
Splish-splash 6
Splosh 40
Squawk 28
Squeaks 10
Squeal 20
Squeee-squeee 20
Squeeeek 10
Sssss 22
Steams 4
Swings 12
Swish-swash 4
Swish-swish 12
Swishes 4
Swoosh 40

T
Thud 32
Thump 32

Tick-tock 4
Ticks 4
Ting-a-ling 14, 16
Tings 16
Tinkle-tinkle 40
Trills 34
Tweet 34

W
Wails 14
Whaa-ooo 38
Whack-whack 22
Whirrr-er 18
Who 24
Whoosh 26
Writes 10

Z
Zzzzzz 6, 40

More Books About Sounds

Here are some more books about sounds. Look at the
list. If you see any books you would like to read,
see if your library or bookstore has them.

All About Sound. Knight (Troll)
A Very Noisy Day. Myller (Atheneum)
Bremen-Town Musicians. Plume (Doubleday)
Country Noisy Book. Brown (Harper & Row)
Crash! Bang! Boom! Spier (Doubleday)
Gobble, Growl, Grunt. Spier (Doubleday)
High Sounds, Low Sounds. Branley (Harcourt Brace
    Jovanovich)
Make Your Own Musical Instruments. Mandell and
    Wood (Harcourt Brace Jovanovich)
Mama Don't Allow. Hurd (Harper Trophy)
Max the Music Maker. Stecher and Kandell
    (Lothrop, Lee & Shepard)
My Five Senses. Aliki (Harper & Row)
Noisy Book. Brown (Harper & Row)
Pigs Say Oink: A First Book of Sounds. Alexander
    (Random House)
Winter Noisy Book. Brown (Harper & Row)

For Grown-ups

Sounds! is a picture book that uses alliteration, onomatopoeia, phonetic spellings of sounds, and rhyme to introduce children to the concept of sounds. The "Index of Sound Words" on page 46 provides a list of all the "sound words" that comprise the bulk of this book's controlled vocabulary text. This index will give educators, librarians, and parents a quick guide to using this book to complement and challenge a young reader's developing language and reading skills.

The editors invite interested adults to examine the sampling of reading level scores at the bottom of this page. Reading level estimates help adults decide what reading materials are appropriate for children at certain grade levels. These estimates are useful because they are usually based on syllable, word, and sentence counts — information that is taken from the text itself.

As useful as reading level scores are, however, we have not slavishly followed the dictates of readability formulas in our efforts to encourage young readers. Most reading specialists agree that reading skill is built on practice in reading, listening, speaking, and drawing meaning from language — activities that adults "do" when they read with children. These factors are not measured by readability scores; and yet they do enhance a text's value and appeal for children at early reading levels.

In *Sounds!,* the "Contents," index, "Things to Talk About," "Things to Do," and "More Books About Sounds" sections help children become good readers by encouraging them to use the words they read as conveyors of meaning, not as objects to be memorized. And these sections give adults a chance to participate in the learning — and enjoyment — to be found in this book.

Reading level analysis: SPACHE 2.9, FRY 1, FLESCH 94 (very easy), RAYGOR 4, FOG 3.5, SMOG 3